How NOT to Manifest

Manifestation Mistakes to AVOID and How to Finally Make LOA Work for You

(or take it to the next level!)

Law of Attraction Short Reads, Book 2

By Elena G. Rivers

Table of Contents

8

Introduction – How Not to Manifest

Are you ready to discover the biggest manifestation mistakes and blocks that most people encounter on their LOA journeys?

Do you want to let go of what's no longer serving you so that you can finally make the law of attraction work for you, not against you? How would it feel to manifest with joy, ease, and confidence, while feeling like an excited kid awaiting a holiday?

The good news is that your life can indeed get super magical if you know how to use the powers of the law of attraction. But, it's not only about what you do, my friend. It's also about how you do it. At the same time, it's also about who you are and who you become.

You see, most people get too fixated on different law of attraction techniques as this is what most LOA teachers tend to focus on exclusively. The concept of self-image and your energy behind your manifestations is still very often overlooked by so many people!

Most people obsess with numerous LOA strategies, desperately searching for that one particular method that will make them successful.

I have nothing against learning new manifestation methods.

To be honest with you, all manifestation methods out there do work, and they work very well if done correctly and with good energy while in alignment with your authentic self. It isn't my intention to criticize other books, teachers, or methods since I firmly believe that most LOA teachers have good intentions and want to help you as much as they can.

However, it's not only about the methods alone (even though they are essential). It's ALL about the person who utilizes those methods. It's about you, your mindset, and, more importantly, your energy!

I create my books to bridge that gap. I help you dive more in-depth, so that you get the tools that allow you to embrace an entirely new mindset and new, super high vibe, "all-blocks-removed" energy.

With the new mindset and energy, you become a new person, almost on autopilot. As such, you suddenly discover that many of the manifestation methods that perhaps didn't work for you in the past, might actually work like magic for you now!

Changing your energy is the real journey of the manifestation and law of attraction. There's nothing more empowering than knowing you can align your self-image with your true desires. What you learn on your journey and who you become in the process is priceless.

Real confidence comes not from believing but from knowing. Knowing who you are and what you can attract in your life! Once you've tapped into your powers, nobody will ever take them away from you, and your life will magically transform.

Yes, there will be some occasional obstacles. But thanks to your new, more empowered self, you'll be able to find solutions to turn the negative into positive mindfully.

If you're new to the law of attraction, this book will help you kick start your journey and potentially avoid years of trial and error, frustration, and disappointment. I want you to manifest with ease and confidence!

At the same time, if you're an experienced "manifestor" and you've already studied LOA for years, I'm positive this little book will help you take it to the next level while making you feel more joyful, lighter, and happier.

This is the side effect of eliminating all the manifestation mistakes and blocks from your life. It's almost like a mental, emotional, and spiritual detox.

For example, if you want to live a healthy lifestyle and change your diet, most nutritionists would first recommend you cleanse your body from toxins, so that you can make the most of your new, healthy diet. A good cleanse can also help your body with nutrient absorption so that your new, healthy lifestyle is more effective.

The same mindset applies to the law of attraction and spirituality. We need to let go of what no longer serves us so that we can make the space for the new – mentally, spiritually, emotionally, and energetically.

One of the most common mistakes people make with LOA is continually looking for new methods...as if the latest was always the solution!

(I have been there myself, so I am not judging, I was the worst, trust me, it can't get worse than my old self!).

Once again, it's not your fault. We're programmed by a society that's run by fear-based marketing. Fear-based marketing always tells us that we aren't good enough unless we get hold of this new thing that will help us transform all areas of our lives in seven seconds or less.

It's a very manipulative marketing tactic, very often abused by fake, hype gurus who want to lure you into their sales funnels with flashy promises of the new: this new thing, this new method!

11

It's no wonder that a soul can get lost in the endless chain of chasing. Now, I'll be the first one to admit that on my journey to mastering the manifestation process, I got sucked into dozens of schemes – both from "spiritual" and "make money fast" gurus.

Remember, my friend; it's not only about chasing "the latest information." It's also about the motivation and inspiration to apply what you already know.

So, am I saying it's wrong to look for new information related to manifestation and law of attraction?

Well, not at all, if you genuinely enjoy learning and filling your mind with positivity. Reading positive, feel-good books like this one can help you raise your vibration almost instantly. So, if you enjoy learning, go for it!

However, always remember to protect and control your mind and never allow dishonest people to take advantage of you by using shame, guilt, and fear-based tactics while telling you aren't good enough as you are.

You're good enough now, and you've always been good enough because you're a part of the divine power. So, get ready to release all your doubts and fears! This book will give you a new perspective on how you can transform your life and shape it according to your genuine and authentic personal desires. The power you can type into is very creative. However, it can only be used for the good. So, never use it to take advantage of others or manipulate them against their will, for your own gain.

Everything can and will unfold to everyone's higher good!

As a light worker turned author, I must shed light on the darkness, so that the real transformation can take place. Hence, this book offers a totally different angle!

As a friend a mine read this book before it was published, she said:

"Hold on a second Elena, you're all about positivity, but the title seems a bit negative to me.

Shouldn't we just focus on the positive? I'm confused. What if people focus on how not to manifest and will never get anywhere?"

Several other people gave me the same feedback. So, to clarify, yes, we should focus on the positive. I am all for the positive and whatever makes us feel good. However, before we do dive into real, authentic positivity, we need to let go of the negative that may be blocking the real, creative, positive flow. The mental, emotional, and spiritual peeling needs to be done so that you can shine your best self and manifest your dream life.

So many people get lost looking for more manifestation methods to try, but they never dive deeper to get rid of what is no longer serving them. This is where I come in with my books. My mission is to help people detox holistically so that they finally let go of mental, spiritual, and emotional patterns that are negative. These negative patterns always result in negative manifestations.

My goal is to help you feel amazing and create a life that exceeds your expectations. Not from fear, not from greed, not to prove other people wrong. I want you to create from a place of joy, natural confidence, and self-love as well as love for other beings. I intend to uplift you and inspire you so that you can transform your life to such an extent that you also uplift and inspire everyone around you!

As a light worker in my core, and the law of attraction author, I want to raise the vibration of the planet.

I am very grateful for you, the Reader. I am thankful you are learning and growing. You trusted me enough to get this book, even though I am not a big LOA guru or a famous brand.

(It isn't my intention anyway, because I don't want to manifest fame, a topic for another day!).

Imagine you are doing a total makeover in your house or apartment. It's logical that before ordering new furniture, you'd want to get rid of the old, right? In the process, you may also realize that some walls need painting and whatnot.

This is precisely how it works with the law of attraction and manifestation process. Most mistakes that people make come from misunderstanding the concept of mindset, energy, and the old emotional baggage and habits that need to go.

Some things are easy to spot and let go of because you are aware of them. Most of the time, these are related to habits and mindset. If you've ever studied any self-help literature, you already understand how the way you think and act can change you and your life.

The deeper stuff remains unseen at first, though. Luckily, energy clearing, as well as understanding deep emotional patterns, can help...

No healing modality is better than others. They all go together. On my journey, I've had the privilege to study Reiki, metaphysics, energy work, chakra balance, EFT (Emotional Freedom Technique), as well as traditional self-help and mindset literature. I also studied business and marketing, which may seem not relevant for most people on this spiritual and manifestation journey.

However, understanding marketing taught me a lot about human psychology as well as fear-based messages that are always around us and can put us in a negative, desperate state.

It's because most marketing campaigns around us (many of them are subliminal) are fear-based, and so we get used to operating from our fears, almost most of the time.

Luckily, there's also loved-based marketing aimed at speaking to your higher self and helping you make decisions based on love, not fear. So, not all marketing is necessarily evil.

Most big companies use fear-based marketing, though, because it generates more sales for them, much faster.

The concept of love and fear-based mindset can also be applied to life; it's not just a marketing and advertising concept. If you dive deep into your past, I'm sure you'll swiftly start noticing some interesting patterns, for example, how the best circumstances you attracted into your life were caused by your loved-based mindset, while operating from a place of love, not fear.

At the same time, you may recognize that if you attracted something negative, it was because of the fear-based mindset that someone forced onto you to make you feel bad.

My combined knowledge from different, very often not related, modalities from marketing to energy work, gave me a new perspective on manifestation, and it's the foundation of all my teachings.

I always ask my readers to think of manifesting in terms of energy, mindset, and strategy. There's no particular order here because everyone is different. So, I won't push you to do things in a specific order, just to get you to do things my way. To understand this more in-depth, you need to continually ask yourself – what do I need to focus on? Is it my mindset, my energy, or my strategy?

The strategy is, as you probably know, the manifestation techniques you have chosen to use. This book will give you plenty of ideas for manifestation methods you can use, so don't worry. I've got you covered, even if you haven't read any other of my books or are new to LOA.

However, there's also your manifestation mindset. It involves your motivation, your discipline, and what drives you. Are you a person who can stick to a manifestation habit and keep going with patience? Do you operate from fear or love? How do you feel and what's going on in your mind?

Finally, your energy- the deep stuff. Getting rid of different layers. Changing your energy and who you are by discovering your true, authentic self and manifesting from a place of love.

Energy work is a beautiful thing, and it can even make you change your manifestation goals. For example, I used to seek fame, success, and recognition. I'd continuously chase the approval from people I didn't even care about. As a result, I lost my true happiness, passion, and fulfilment.

I was so obsessed with what others thought of me, and what others believed I should do, that I neglected my true calling for a very long time.

So, back then, I did manifest from that place of misery, and I manifested a profitable business that was totally out of alignment with who I was. It further exhausted me, my health, and my personal life.

During that time, my proud ego was telling me that I could manifest with ease and that I was better than everyone else because I was so smart. I could have a lucrative business and a fantastic lifestyle with exotic travels! While my Facebook and Instagram friends thought I "made it," deep inside, I was very miserable.

After some initial success of my old manifestations, something terrible would always happen. From dishonest accountants and business partners to adrenal exhaustion, very negative clients, unexpected refunds, and very negative thoughts. I still kept thinking:

"Oh, but my mindset and strategy are so good. It's all about the mindset and strategy!!! I know I can make money, and this is what I wanted, right?"

So, I got stuck in this "smart mindset" and "hustle strategy." I forgot about my energy, though.

Yes, both mindset and strategy are essential, and they're all you need if you are already operating from a place of love, your vibration is high, and you don't manifest to prove others wrong or to show off. If your energy is in place, then yes, mindset and strategy will follow to your advantage.

But, in my case, well, what can I say! My old self needed some energy work. So, I got started on EFT (Emotional Freedom Technique) and Reiki.

Eventually, through my consistency and commitment to these amazing energy and emotional health modalities, I completely changed my life, created my reality, and stopped chasing superficial goals. I became a new person!

And so, here I come now – a woman with many interests, a weird mixture of a writer, light worker, business owner, marketing nerd, and manifestation freak, with a passion for energy work and law of attraction.

The darkest period of my life turned out to be the biggest blessing and the strongest catalyst on my journey. I had to let go of the old, let go of my old ways, my old business. I had to stop chasing! I became a new person, and as such, I began manifesting my reality from a completely new paradigm.

Don't forget; everything is interconnected. I often see that people want to manifest, and all they focus on are manifestation techniques or everything with "manifestation" and "law of attraction" in it.

Anything else, such as any other healing modality, they reject (once again, not judging, since I've been there myself).

However, learning more about yourself, your deep motivation, how to master your emotions, your discipline, and, most importantly, your subconscious mind while releasing all those negative blocks can be the best manifestation method! Trust me on that one.

It'll work much better long term, much better than blindly reciting affirmations or mindlessly writing in your journal. Don't get me wrong, I'm not bashing affirmations or writing them down.

But it's not only about what you do and not even about how you do it. It's also about how you feel and who you are.

I once spent over 200 bucks on a book that told me to write my money goals down and recite them. Yes, it's not an editing error, the book was expensive! Now, it isn't my intention to blame the book. Apparently, its techniques did work for some people who followed it.

However, I can take responsibility here and will expose my old self. Not from a place of guilt, but a place of relief, knowing that now, I'm a new person and can manifest from that new space and new energy.

First of all, I got that 200 dollar book from a place of deep fear, shame, and guilt. My business at the time was slow; it wouldn't grow; I didn't hit my goals even though I worked very hard.

I was going to travel to an expensive business mastermind and was ashamed that other business owners had more success than I did. Not the best situation and mindset to manifest from a place of love!

It would've been better to invest in that book from a place of love and curiosity, such as: *"Let' see if I can have fun with this, let's see if some mental blocks come up as I do this exercise, hmm, let's see if the Universe thinks it's the right time for me to manifest, or perhaps it wants to test me for now.*

But, at that time, I was in a very negative and desperate mindset.

So, I was doing what that book taught me, all from a place of lack and shame. I also hired a business mentor (from the same negative energy), and at that time, it was one of the worst business decisions I have made. As a consequence, my revenue, instead of going up, went down, and I only began manifesting more expenses. My health deteriorated, and I felt so burned out, I couldn't even get out of bed.

At first, I was in a victim mindset and blamed the mentors and also the book I'd bought. But then, I deeply explored my energy and asked myself:

"Elena, why the heck did you attract those people into your life? What was your real motivation? To manifest money fast, just to maintain your success status of a high-income earner? Do you even care about such a status?"

Then, the answers came to me, and I knew I had to change pretty much everything in my life. I attracted what I didn't want because I wasn't myself. I wasn't my true, authentic self.

No wonder it didn't work. Once again, to make it clear for you, my reader, this is a true story from my life, and I don't share it to complain or to be negative. I've done lots of mindset and energy work since then, so now, I can just share my story without any feelings of blame and guilt attached to it. Hopefully, you can learn from it. I don't want you to suffer as my old self did!

It just happened; it just was. It was my old self and my old reality. I am grateful for it, though, because it helped me change my relationship with LOA and gave me a new perspective.

That new perspective is the real, authentic foundation for everything I share and for all the books I write.

I don't write for fame and recognition. I want to stay behind the scenes because it allows me to focus intensely on writing, research, and serving my readers, all while maintaining a life-work balance.

Also, I'm not a perfect guru, and I don't claim I know it all. But what I do know, I love to share with honesty and transparency. My sincere intention is to help you think for yourself and help you get rid of all the harmful programs that are not yours, so that you can embrace your true, authentic self and manifest from there.

I write feel-good books, from a place of love; however, I'm not a fan of fluffy books with no substance.

All my books are short and practical, leaving the reader with easy-to-apply and flexible ideas. I don't believe in one-size-fits-all self-help or manifestation systems. What you need is to create your own system. The books I write are designed as tools and inspiration to help you do so.

Everyone is different. As a general rule of all my teachings, it's always the mix of your mindset, energy, and strategy. You need to maintain the balance between the three, just like you need to keep the balance between the action and attraction, the masculine and feminine.

I write feel-good books, always from a place of love, but since honesty is one of my most significant values, sometimes my love can be a bit of tough love. Once again-only for the highest good!

I write in a conversational style as if I was talking to you over a nice cup of coffee. It isn't my intention to become an award-winning writer (nothing wrong with that if that's your goal). Instead, I want to create books that are easy to read and easy to absorb (so that they can also help people who aren't native English speakers or don't have higher education).

I don't want you to worship me, or idolize me. I keep my private life – private. I've already shared enough about myself in the intro of this book, so that you understand how your manifestation process can shift if you work on your mindset and energy. You now also know why I do what I do and how it may be a bit different compared to what you've already been studying.

(I'm not asserting that what you've been studying or doing is wrong, because I have this "new system." You already know I'm against fear-based tactics).

I don't have any agenda. From my experience (and yes, I studied marketing as a part of my spiritual journey, as weird as it may seem!), sticking to an agenda can drain one's energy (and kill trust and authenticity). I care about my energy and your energy, as well. I write for ambitious souls, and so I know that my readers can make their judgments and decisions. I'm fine if they don't agree with everything I say.

It isn't my goal to influence, convince, or convert you.

Talking about "converting you" - there's no high-end program attached to this book because this book already contains everything you need to know about manifestation mistakes to avoid, how not to manifest and what you need to focus on to create your dream reality. So, there's no "cliff-hanger" or an upsell in this book.

I don't have any further "backend" offer in this book (if I had one, I'd be honest about it from the beginning!).

So, you can relax, this booklet has all you need for now. I encourage you to read with an open mind. Read and re-read several times, if needed. Don't focus on everything at once. Follow your intuition.

Trust me, amazing things will happen. I'm very excited for you!

Love,

Elena

Free LOA Newsletter + Bonus Gift

Before we dive into the contents of this book, I'd like to offer you a free copy of my **LOA Workbook — *a powerful, FREE 5-day program (eBook & audio)*** designed to help you raise your vibration while eliminating resistance and negativity.

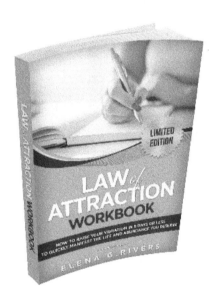

To sign up for free, visit the link below now:

www.loaforsuccess.com/newsletter

You'll also get free access to my highly acclaimed, uplifting LOA Newsletter.

Through this email newsletter, I regularly share all you need to know about the manifestation mindset and energy.

My newsletter alone helped hundreds of my readers manifest their own desires.

Plus, whenever I release a new book, you can get it at a deeply discounted price or even for free.

You can also start receiving my new audiobooks published on Audible at no cost!

To sign up for free, visit the link below now:

www.loaforsuccess.com/newsletter

I'd love to connect with you and stay in touch with you while helping you on your LOA journey!

■ ■

If you happen to have any technical issues with your sign up, please email us at:

support@LOAforSuccess.com

Chapter 1 Make LOA Easier for You Right Here, Right Now!

Success starts with awareness, so we need to be keenly aware of old patterns.

One of the best ways to become aware of any patterns in your life is to become, what I like to call, your own Law of Attraction Detective.

From my experience (and after talking to hundreds of LOA practitioners, teachers, and students), I can tell you that your higher self has all the answers you need. The more authentic intentions you set, the deeper you can get into your unique solutions and manifest with ease.

My *Law of Attraction Detective* process is simple. I want to know both my negative as well as positive patterns, so that I can let go of the negative and focus on the positive. In other words, you need to have an honest look at your life and analyse both the good and the bad that you attracted. This is how you can reverse engineer your success (or the lack of it) and be your own manifestation guru!

It's lots of fun, and it shows that you can be your own therapist and coach as well. So, this is how I do it. It's a process I like getting back to every few months or so.

As a real "journaling junkie," I'm also looking for an excuse to get another notebook or a journal, haha!

(I like to use different journals for different purposes. Works well for me!)

While I don't want to say that I first focus on the negative, it's kind of what I do to begin this process. However, it's not what it seems, because I don't dwell on any negative events from my past. For me, it's all about looking for patterns and then mindfully letting them go!

I've already shared my story in the introduction of this book, so there is no point in repeating it. What I do, is I mindfully detect on the negative thoughts and feelings that were accompanying me when the negative manifestation happened.

I write in my journal:

I choose to let go of fear, self-guilt, jealousy, judgment, and chasing success to prove others wrong.

I choose to let go of impatience.

I choose to let go of negative people that no longer serve me!

As I keep writing, more negative patterns keep coming, so I keep writing them down to make sure I let them go:

I choose to let go of dishonest people.

I choose to let go of gossip.

I choose to let go of blame.

I no longer criticize other people.

Whatever comes to your mind, write it down!

Now that we've mindfully erased the negative, let's focus on the positive! The best thing you can do is to re-write your negative patterns and make them positive.

Now, I am patient. Now, I trust the process.

Now, I LOVE myself.

Now, I attract honest and loving people.

Now, I search for information because I LOVE learning.

I no longer need to prove anything, because as a child of God, I am already good enough.

Just keep writing!

If you meditate on a regular basis, you may start to receive downloads, that will give you more information about the negative patterns to release and re-write.

(If you don't meditate, don't worry about it for now; it's not a step required in this process, you can get started on meditation whenever you want, and all the information about your negative patterns will also come to light, so that you can heal).

Now, the final step is to reflect on all the good things, people, and circumstances you've attracted so far. Ask yourself, what you did and how you felt. Start looking for positive patterns and write them down.

For me, personally, I've manifested the best things into my life (sometimes even unexpected things), after committing to:

-daily gratitude

-laughter

-love and helping others

-letting go of trying to prove myself

-letting go of seeking approval

-doing what I love, as much as I can (doing your passion, can put you into a high vibration!)

-practicing EFT (Emotional Freedom Technique)

-reading positive books and articles written by people with no agenda

-letting go of the outcome and being OK with not achieving my goal (while mindfully doing the best I can, right here, and right now, with a sincere intention to learn and expand!).

So, this is how I reverse engineer what worked and what didn't work to unleash the negative and positive patterns. It's like a diet plan for the soul. You let go of the foods that make you sick and stick to the foods that make you vibrant.

If you don't feel like writing, I highly recommend you at least start reflecting on your past experiences. The best time for reflection is when you feel deeply relaxed.

(I'll offer more on relaxation in the following chapters; deep relaxation can do real wonders to your manifesting abilities).

For some people, it may be going to a spa or taking an Epsom salt bath at home. Others may benefit from walking on the beach, in the forest, or some beautiful location. Some may just want to lie down with some nice incense sticks and a cup of green tea.

However, when it comes to patterns, the most important thing is your awareness. In the process of transitioning to a new, more empowered version of yourself, you may catch yourself following back into some old negative patterns. If that's the case, remember, you aren't alone! We all tend to get trapped in old emotions and feelings.

What's genuinely liberating is the fact that what can set us free is some good, old-fashioned strong-will, combined with mindfulness. If you find yourself falling back into negativity, just take a few deep breaths, close your eyes, and visualize a big red stop sign. Then, tell yourself: *"It's OK, you've got this! It's time to move on and let go!"*

The more you do it, the easier it gets. Remember, don't beat yourself up for falling back into the old patterns because you can always choose to get up, brush yourself off, and stick to the new, more empowered version of yourself.

Now, let's focus on one crucial tip, something I like to call the Deadly LOA Sin.

And, the deadly sin is....

Being too attached to the outcome!

Remember my story?

-mindlessly writing my money goals in my journal

-mindlessly investing in some mentors without doing any research on them,

-desperate to manifest more revenue in my old business- fast, so that I could show off to people I didn't care about anyway... (and they didn't care about me).

Well, more often than not, desperation will act against us. Perhaps you have even experienced it yourself?

Just analyse your life and all the decisions you made out of fear or some weird need to please others. How did that end? What did you manifest? Was it right for you and your wellbeing in the long run?

It all comes down to letting go of the outcome while focusing on the process itself and just enjoying who you're becoming as you get closer to your goals.

Letting go of the outcome is hard in the beginning, but with more awareness on your part, your "let go of the outcome" muscle will be created. Personally, what I like to do is to ask myself, what's the worst thing that can happen if I don't manifest my desire now?

For example, as I'm writing this book, the worst thing that can happen is that very few people will take an interest in it. But, even with such a scenario, I see myself as a winner. Why? Well, because I'll have another book published. That alone is very therapeutic for me. And even if just one person gets inspired by it, it's a massive win for both of us!

At the same time, with each book I write, I improve my skills and practice for "the bigger show." It's all about learning. So, even if this book doesn't hit the bestseller lists, it's OK. I can't fail because I succeed or I learn. If this book doesn't do as well as I intend it to be, then it'll be the next one. I know that the Universe can see much more than I do; and I understand that as long as I can communicate with it, from a place of love and real, authentic intention, while putting in meaningful and inspired action, I'll manifest my desires. If not now, then next time. I'm not going anywhere, and I'm very excited to see how this book series will unfold. Perhaps the Universe wants me to write dozens or hundreds of books? We'll see.

So, this is the thought process I go through to reduce my attachment to the outcome. At the same time, I remain open to manifesting my intention from other sources of creative self-expression because I trust that the Universe knows what is better for my long-term wellbeing and success. I release the grip of control. I put in the work (doing what I love), I learn, and I just know I'll get there. I don't even need to believe, I know.

It's like watching your favorite TV show that airs at a certain time; you know you'll watch it, right? Even if you miss it this week, you'll catch up next week. You don't need to believe it because you know you'll watch it and have fun with it.

Well, that's the vibe we want to embrace, my friend!

Perhaps you've noticed that some people always TRY to win the lottery or always TRY to meet their soulmate, and they are so attached to the specific way or specific person, that it makes them needy. Aside from the fact that they get stuck in trying and wanting, there's also lots of negative energy of attachment created in the process. It has to be now, and it has to be fast, and oh you've gotta believe hard! Once again, nothing wrong with believing if you believe from a place of happiness, love, and wholeness.

But, neediness and attachment need to go! And, it's much more empowering to be open to different sources of delivery. For example, a person may be holding on to manifesting more abundance through a salary raise. However, at the same time, they may remain closed to manifesting the same abundance through other channels. Perhaps there's some investment opportunity or an interesting part-time business idea. But they reject it and never look into it because they get too fixated on the specific revenue of manifesting the abundance they desire.

(Just like a person may get stuck trying to manifest a specific person into one's life while ignoring other amazing people that could have been a better match)

So, be open-minded while manifesting! Sure, have your preferred channel or manifestation preference, if needed. But, set the intention to be open to other channels as well. You never know what the Universe holds in store for you, so be ready to move on fast and let go of the old, when applicable.

Have you ever been on a date with someone who was just way too needy? How did that work out? You probably found such a person repelling. Well, this is how the Universe may feel if you get too needy, so, once again, relax the grip.

Finally, be prepared for some challenges and roadblocks as you manifest. Please note, I'm not saying it has to be hard every time, or do I encourage you to focus on those challenges and invite them into your life. But, once again, your current state of awareness may not understand the bigger picture yet, so trust the Universe. Whenever there's a roadblock or a challenge, see it as a test that the Universe is sending you just to see how strong your desire is. You can always control your perception!

For example, several months ago, I had to go on sick leave, and at first, I felt very sorry for myself. Initially, it was the lockdown, and one of my businesses got affected. As if it wasn't enough, I got sick and had to take some time off. But then, I reminded myself that things happen for me, not to me. In alignment with that, I decided to enjoy my sick leave and use it as a time to slow down. I realized that I hadn't taken a vacation in a long time, and my body and mind probably rebelled, so I manifested a disease to protect myself from burnout.

Instead of worrying and complaining, I decided to dive into my time off mindfully. Instead of calling it "sick leave," I called it a Deep Healing and Mindset Makeover Leave.

During my break, I spent days looking at the ocean, cooking and eating healthy nutritious food, making healthy smoothies, watching comedies, laughing, and listening to inspiring videos and audiobooks. I realized that life isn't only about money and success.

During one of my meditations, a powerful download came to me: *It was all meant to happen, because it's a part of the process!*

I decided to switch off all the negativity that was going on around me, and I focused my energy on healing. Eventually, I decided to let go of one of my businesses as I realized it wasn't my passion nor a long-term path.

So, my initial challenge, such as losing sales due to the global pandemic and getting sick, was a good thing! By letting go of that old business, now I can focus on writing more books, which is my true passion. I can create a new chapter in my life, all because I reframed what happened to me into something positive.

Labels and roadblocks can help you; just see them more holistically. Not all things that you think are bad for you now are bad for you long term. Always look for something good; always seek something to be grateful for. If you can't find it yourself, or you feel alone, talk to a friend, or find some positive LOA groups online. Never suffer alone!

As you practice your "it happened for me, not to me" muscle, you'll be able to magically transform your life with gratitude and transform negativity into positivity.

To sum up this chapter: by being too attached to the result and the source of your manifestation (or a particular person), you limit other revenues of receiving. You don't want to get caught up in a vicious cycle of "I'll be happy when..." You want to be happy now!

Focus on your state of being and your happiness first.

Target your emotions attached to your intention.

Emotions we feel can help us go where we want to go or separate us from our manifestation. Be honest with yourself and ask yourself: *Am I feeling whole and complete now? Am I feeling well taken care of?*

Don't train your brain to look for opportunities that make you feel like you're far away and separate from your goal. A good example would be: *"I feel lonely, and I can't love myself, so I want to manifest that person to love me, so that I can feel good."*

That's a big no-no!

Or: *I feel I'm not worthy and deserving. I feel like I'm not good enough. I need to manifest millions of dollars first, and only then will I feel worthy of doing what I love.*

Once again, this logic is a big no-no!

As Neville Guard says, "the feeling is the secret".

Good feelings are the foundation of everything you do.

It's easier said than done, right?

Well, this chapter is called the way it's called for a reason because I know that the information I share can help you, my friend.

Your brain wants to feel safe and secure and as far away from the new as possible. However, by aligning yourself with good feelings, you make your mind understand that what you intend to manifest is safe. Allow yourself to experience the feeling of love and abundance now. Encourage yourself to be whole and complete now, even if you won't manifest your intentions fast, or an unexpected challenge comes, be OK with the process. Know that everything is unfolding as it should!

Don't be so serious about your goal, since it may hold you back from the feeling. Whenever you catch yourself being too much in your head, focus on your heart. Transition out of your head and into your heart! Take a few deep breaths while placing your hands on your heart and just breathe in and out. Your heart knows! It doesn't plot against you, and it doesn't overthink. Do this whenever you feel anxious.

Schedule daily activities that make you feel happy, genuinely happy. You like swimming, it makes you feel free? Well, go swimming! You love dancing and singing? Do it. Feel like the new, more empowered version of yourself NOW. Have fun!

For example, you intend to manifest a new business or a job. Maybe you want to manifest a life partner. Loosen up and understand you can generate the emotion right here right now. Also, what you currently know and understand and consider as your truth and the only path to your manifestation, may be limited. Perhaps the Universe understands your need better than you do and wants to give you a better deal?

Also, remember that you always manifest. Most people overlook it as they often get too caught up in what they don't have. Give yourself more credit for all the good things you have already manifested into your life.

And what about today? Well, you're still alive. You've manifested this book. If you're reading this book on any digital device, well, you could afford it, or someone lent it to you. Either way, you manifested it so that you can now enjoy this book! Oh, and you can read because you can see. If you're wearing glasses or contact lenses, once again, they were made for you, someone's invention helps you see better.

You always manifest those little great things, so stay in a positive mindset!

To sum up, this chapter, let's focus on a few questions I got from our readers. It's much easier to understand how LOA works if you can follow real-life examples, questions that readers ask me, and my answers. Who knows? Maybe we're even reading your mind, perhaps you have the same questions already?

The following are some questions and answers from my email newsletter readers.

Question:

Hello Elena,

I have a question: how can I visualize to experience a positive feeling and let go at the same time? For example, when I focus on visualizing, doesn't it make me naturally think of different manifestation possibilities and feeling too attached to the outcome as a result? How do I create a decent balance between the two? Can you please advise? Thank you!

Answer:

Yes, there are many ways to create balanced visualizations, so that you can align yourself with the feeling, without creating the resistance.

I'd suggest you focus on the larger ideas, and the real essence behind what you want. For example, if you want a beautiful new house, don't just think about it and what it would look like. Be sure to catch yourself whenever your mind starts complaining that you don't have it yet, as that would be getting too attached to the outcome. At the same time, be very mindful of all those negative voices such as "this is not for me, how can I even afford it with my current salary".

If any negativity or overthinking come as you visualize, just take a few deep breaths and let go by saying: "OK, thank you my old self, it's time to move on because now I feel worthy."

Focus on what it'd feel like walking around your new house, cook in your new kitchen or sleep in your new bedroom. Also, focus on the feeling of what that new house really represents.

Deep inside, you may not care that much about some house design or a trendy floor. So, what does the new house represent to you? Is it security, comfort, freedom, belonging, taking care of yourself, and others?

Focus on the feelings and don't overthink all the details about what needs to be done for you to get the house. Unexpected ideas will eventually pop into your head as you stick to the process. Then, be sure to take action on your new ideas.

Also, use this exercise to let go of any negative feelings, such as wanting to manifest out of jealousy for what other people have, or to show off. Trust me, I've made such a mistake in the past and all my manifestations that came, as a result, were very short-term and not good for my energy, success, and wellbeing.

Another brilliant idea is to use creative visualization to stretch your mindset and let go of fears and doubts. I have a simple, mindfulness-based exercise that can help you do so. Let's stick to the idea of your new house for a while. You can visualize your bank account with a large sum of money. Be very mindful of different feelings that pop into your mind as *you do so. For example, some feelings could be negative, such us: "Oh, but what happens if I lose that money I saved and have to start from scratch?"*

Take a few deep breaths and let go. Understand that as an owner of such a beautiful home, it's easy and natural for you to attract large sums of money so that you can quickly pay off your house. It's as easy as buying a cup of coffee.

Once again, you can't go wrong with this visualization, because if any negativity crops up, you can be mindful about it and let it go. You can easily catch your old self and your old patterns.

Perhaps you start thinking: "Oh, now I have to pay this property tax!" And once again, let go. The new version of yourself that already lives in that beautiful house can easily pay any property tax; it's as easy as paying for lunch or coffee.

And yes, buying a cup of coffee is easy. Even if a place where you buy coffee screws it up, you could get over a few bucks, because for you it's just a few bucks. But a person who lives in an impoverished country has a different perception of those few bucks that you can easily afford to lose on a coffee.

As you dive deep into your thoughts and mind, you'll be able to spot many interesting patterns. Keep affirming that it's safe for you to manifest that new house. And that the current home you live in is a great step forward!

I hope this helps. I highly recommend you explore my ideas and stick to what works for you and what makes you feel good because your way is always better than my way. It has to be your way because it's your energy and your manifestation

Chapter 2 Eliminating Your Fear of Success to Help You Shine

In the last chapter, we mentioned the fear of failure and reducing the importance by understanding how challenges can help us.

We also know that we can't fail! We succeed, or we learn. Everything is unfolding just like it should, so don't get stuck in any negative judgments.

However, there's also one manifestation mistake that I like to call the Invisible Manifestation Enemy and to be quite frank, very few LOA gurus talk about it.

So, what is this "invisible enemy?" Well, it's the fear of success, yes! We may subconsciously fear expansion and success.

However, once again, there's no need to worry because, more often than not, those fears of success mean that we are good people, and we don't want to make others feel bad, inferior, or intimidated by our success.

One significant mindset shift is to remind yourself that you achieve success and manifest your desires not to make other people feel inadequate or inferior. You don't manifest from a place of superiority but a place of empowerment.

As you manifest your success, a success that's in alignment with who you are, people who are ready to evolve will get inspired by it; and that will allow them to manifest their desires, too. See your end result as empowerment instead of something others will want to steal from you or deprive you of.

One of my friends wanted to launch her side business for years...yet she always felt stuck and had excuses. She procrastinated and felt terrible about it.

After going through the material covered in this book, she finally realized what was holding her back. She was afraid that with her business, she'd be making more money than her husband and that he'd leave her because of that.

The realization came straight out of her subconscious mind, as she was eliminating her manifestation blocks, following this book.

(I'll show you a very practical way to help you "cleanse out" all the negative blocks from your energy field in the following chapters).

For years, she had no idea, even though she was working with a life coach and a therapist. Everyone thought it was the confidence or motivation issue. Maybe she had no idea how to market herself?

And she felt too afraid to share her ideas with her husband also, because deep inside she thought it'd hurt him. Can you believe it?!

Luckily, it's all good now. What happened is that after shifting her personality and energy, she took action to start her side business.

Finally, taking action was not a problem; she just felt like doing it. She enjoyed it. Her husband loved the idea, by the way. Eventually, her company took off, and now she runs it together with her husband, who felt very relieved he could change his career. Everyone is happy!

I've witnessed many transformations like the one above. It's not even about a person making more money. It's about profound change and releasing all the negative patterns that are holding you back from living your life to the fullest.

Whatever happened to you, don't worry. Whatever your background is, I believe in you; you can do this!

Maybe you're like me, the first one in your family to take charge of the money mindset, so that you can create more abundance into your life?

It's so amazing! You're breaking old patterns in your family and creating a new path for the new generation. I'm so proud of you.

Never feel ashamed for intending to manifest more money, personal success, and abundance! Money in itself isn't harmful if used by a good person with good intentions. So, striving for financial success, if that's your goal, isn't the same as being greedy, and you can also use financial abundance to help other people and be of service to your community.

This book will show you how to "naturally fix" your mindset, change your story, and become a new person. That new person, let's call him or her *The Reader 2.0*, will have a totally new self-image.

That new self-image will be aligned to your vision and what you want in life. What's hard for you now is simple, easy, and NORMAL for *The Reader 2.0*.

Just move forward with conviction and confidence!

Now, let me give you a practical Q& A example of someone who identified that fear of success might be holding him or her back.

I remember one of my newsletter subscribers wrote me saying:

Hello Elena,

First of all, thank you for sharing your emails, very inspiring. I never thought about the fear of success until today. Your email really got me thinking about it.

So, my situation is – I used to work in sales and always did well as a salesperson. Last year, I switched to my own business as a spiritual advisor for professional women.

So now, I sell for myself, not for other people. But for some reason, I struggle with sales! It's not the lack of skills, because I was in professional sales for 30 years, always one of the best saleswomen in all the companies I'd worked for formerly.

But now, for some weird reason, in my own business, something often blocks me whenever I talk to my prospects or clients. It's like now; I'm afraid of making offers, even though I know I have amazing programs that can help my clients.

Your information made me realize it may be a fear of success, because if I became a big personal brand or a highly acclaimed expert in my field, someone might start to get jealous or negative energy may be created. I'd be scared that someone would want to destroy me and my success, so maybe, because of that, I choose to limit my flow of abundance by avoiding exposure and not marketing myself enough?

Do you have any tips to help me remove the fear of success? I want to grow my business and serve my clients. But, I also fear it! I have no idea what to do now: I feel scared and, on many occasions, I feel like cancelling calls with clients, or I want to stay in bed.

Answer:

Congrats on your remarkable achievements and the inner work you did. I'm sure you'll be able to help a lot of people because you know how to dive deep and aren't afraid of doing spiritual work on yourself. That makes you a great coach! As you can see, we're already transforming what you perceive as negative into positive, while getting to your authentic core.

First of all, don't be so hard on yourself. Transitioning to running your own business means operating from a new paradigm, and so you may need more time to truly adapt to it while enjoying the process.

Remember, the power is with you already! You can easily reverse engineer what worked for you in the past. Focus on your success in your old company. Working in sales for so many years, and being one of the best is a truly remarkable achievement. Go back there and focus on that feeling of confidence and predictability.

Now, imagine you're driving a car. In the US and most countries in Europe, the driver's seat is on the left, and you drive on the right. But, in the UK, Australia, India, and some other countries, it's the other way round- you sit on the right and drive on the left.

You already have the skill that can allow you to manifest abundance while helping other people. Or, following our above metaphor, you know how to drive, so now you just have to switch to the other side!

The fear of success may appear because you care about your reputation, and you want to help your clients. Through your writing, I can sense you may subconsciously fear being attacked as a famous brand or a public figure.

That fear can be reduced if you focus on your clients, their needs, and fears. Also, create an affirmation that it's safe for you to grow and expand in alignment with who you really are.

And yes, some people may criticize you.

For example, as an author, I know that some people may not like my book (it used to hold me back in the past).

But, sometimes, critics can also offer honest and valuable feedback so, in the end, they are positive in my mind. They give me ideas to improve what I do. In some cases, though, people who criticize are simply in a dark place, and so these also inspire me to do my work to help shift the vibration of the planet.

Either way, my dear, we're good to go!

For more profound healing, I'd recommend you work with a healer such as energy healing, Reiki or EFT (Emotional Freedom Technique) or even a therapist and have a look at your childhood, not to dwell too much on it, but to let go of some old negative subconscious patterns.

Perhaps you did something amazing, excelled at something, and then, someone did not appreciate it? If yes, clear that negative energy, let go, and you'll be healed for life.

It may also be a part of your brand story that will help and inspire other people. I am sure that as a spiritual mentor who works with professional women, having the skill to remove the fear of success can be a niche in itself.

So once again, it's a part of your journey, your story and everything is unfolding as it should.

Now...how about someone who wants to manifest body transformation, a healthy lifestyle, or permanent weight loss? I used to be that somebody. What was holding me back was the fear of success because I didn't want to make my family feel bad.

Knowing what I know now, I understand why it was happening. Back then, I was in self-hate and self-doubt mindset, and I'd allow other people to create labels for me. I didn't dare to disobey; neither did I have the courage to transform on my own terms.

So, this is how it all started. My limiting beliefs about health and fitness originated from my childhood. In my family, nobody was healthy, and many of my family members would laugh at people who jogged or got involved in any healthy activities. My grandpa would always say, "Oh those people have too much free time on their hands, maybe they aren't working? When do they take care of their children?"

So, my limiting belief got a substantial consolidation (and as a result, I subconsciously feared succeeding with weight loss and health as that would mean rejection for me).

If you work out, you don't take enough care of your family.

If you work out too much, you aren't a good person.

Working out is a waste of time.

If you eat healthily, it's too expensive, and if you spend money on expensive stuff, you aren't a good person.

Nobody will like you if they see how much money you spend.

They'll no longer connect with you.

You'll die anyway; you don't need to eat any healthy stuff.

That resulted in massive resistance. Several years ago, I still struggled with eating healthily, and I couldn't lose weight.

I tried different things but could never commit to a healthy lifestyle.

It took me a while to understand where my limiting beliefs were coming from and why they were forming.

But you and I know it's all a process. It's deep work that we're doing here.

Let's get back to my limiting beliefs. Once I'd learned how to gradually get rid of them without feeling self-guilt and without feeling like a victim, I also understood that what very often holds people back isn't the limiting beliefs themselves.

Very often, it's their feeling guilty about having them. Or creating another limiting belief: *I have a limiting belief, and this is who I am, and I don't know how to get rid of it.*

The moment you start putting other *I can't* and *I don't know how's* on what is already stopping you from shining your light and reaching your full potential; you make it harder and harder.

However, once you understand the mechanism behind getting rid of limiting beliefs, you can easily apply it to all the areas of your life. This is exactly what I did. I started with health and fitness. I realized that area needed most of my attention as I was transforming. I also knew that by creating a healthy lifestyle, I could resort to natural methods that would help me soothe the pain, feel less anxiety, sleep better, and eat healthier.

I quickly identified all those negative voices in my head as well as the limiting beliefs that were pretty much coming from other people and were installed on my "hard drive."

But here's the caveat: you cannot just remove a limiting belief and hope for the best. You need to replace the limiting belief with an empowering belief.

For example, the beliefs I got from my family:

- *If you work out, you don't have the time for your family.*
- *Eating healthily is only for rich people.*
- *Eating healthily doesn't taste good anyway, come on, you gotta have something good in your life. Life is already hard enough.*

I began replacing these with self-love and empowerment, one by one. For example, instead of, "If you're always working out, you don't have the time for the family," I said, "You can both work out and hang out with the family and friends."

I began organizing hiking trips that were fun. I could invite some of my friends and family members. We would just walk in nature, burn calories, and have fun. We could still catch up, but instead of going to a bar, we'd get some fresh air, admire nature or even join a yoga workshop. Then, eventually, we felt inspired to combine our hikes with eating healthy food.

Aside from that, I realized that health is the most valuable asset we have. I can still remember what it felt like when I couldn't get up and felt absolutely powerless. The doctors would just prescribe antidepressants, but the truth is, my body lacked a healthy, clean diet and exercise.

Now, I've never been a gym person. So, I decided to focus on other activities, mostly in nature, like hiking, for example. Then I also joined yoga and Pilates classes. I added more positive changes gradually. I kept track of my progress.

I still allowed myself to get off track now and then. That's absolutely fine. You don't want to be too strict on yourself. It's better to focus on your long-term vision.

Eventually, I started enjoying my hikes so much. Getting outdoors in the fresh air just felt amazing. I loved my hikes so much that I decided to take them to another level, and I began jogging. Another change and shift added gradually. Had I vowed to jog every day at the beginning of my journey, I wouldn't have had any success with it. I would've worked on will power alone. And that can only last so long.

So, this is what I did to overcome the fear of success in the area of my life that really needed improvement. And I didn't make anyone feel bad; it was all in my head. My family got inspired by my transformation and now they're also into manifesting health.

Very often, getting rid of your limiting beliefs and fear of success (as well as the fear of failure, as was discussed in the last chapter) alone can be sufficient to manifest. There are a lot of people who manifest easily without using vision boards, without affirming and even without visualizing or knowing a lot about LOA. They manifest because they know how to remove their fears, doubts, and other negative spiritual, emotional, and mental blocks that can drastically slow down or limit any positive manifestation.

Another interesting phenomenon I've observed on my journey is energy work itself. I remember during my Reiki training, fellow Reiki students would manifest things such as an unexpected call with a new job offer, unexpected tax refunds, or a call from someone who wanted to apologize and make things right. The reason for it is deep energy work combined with letting go and then a very deep vibrational shift.

I always was astounded by this amazing energetic phenomenon and after diving deeper (I mean talking to hundreds of people who work in the energy work field, from Reiki, to Feng Shui), I began noticing patterns that I'm now very excited to be sharing with you.

However, very often, a simple relaxation exercise can be enough. Here's what happened to me yesterday:

I was in a restaurant with my partner, and just before our meal, I looked at my phone. I noticed a message from a family member who tends to be very negative. He was asking me some questions about the business I'm no longer in currently. Somehow it connected me to my old self and gave me a negative feeling.

I just gave him a short and polite answer, saying I could no longer help because I've changed my path. Next, I switched off my phone, and desperately tried to focus on my meal. I also felt very thirsty, extremely thirsty, so I ordered more water and then even more water.

My partner noticed I wasn't feeling well, and I just said it was because of the heat probably. Then, when I wanted to pay, suddenly my credit card stopped working! I had no idea why because I had the funds, and it was working perfectly well in the morning. So, I told my partner to wait and went to the nearest cash machine. The card got rejected! I went to another cash machine, and it got rejected again. It said: We cannot perform this operation now.

So, finally, we paid with my partner's credit card, which did work but at the third attempt. Perhaps, he was getting some of my negative energy as well.

I quickly put two and two together and knew I had to shift my energy because I just felt negative. So, when we returned home, the first thing I did was to check with my bank, and they said the card should be working; they saw no reason why it wouldn't be working and advised me to check again. They suggested perhaps it got damaged.

I put on some relaxing music, set a timer for half an hour, and told my partner I needed to relax and let go of negative energy, and so I did. I focused on breathing, intuitively massaging my face, tensing my muscles, and then relaxing them.

I immediately felt good, uplifted, and no longer felt bad about that text message. In fact, I rechecked my phone, and the family member no longer seemed so negative.

Then, I went shopping and decided to try the same credit card again, and I swear to God it worked! It actually worked both in the cash machine and at the shopping mall.

So, this is what energy can do. You may choose to believe or not to believe, but trust me, when you focus on your energy, everything else will go much better, and you will feel better. I recommend you create your own energy work process and do whatever makes you feel relaxed!

Chapter 3 Making the Process Feel Like Having Fun at a Luxury Restaurant

Have fun with your life while you're mindfully waiting for what's yet to come. You've just ordered your meal at the restaurant. Why stress out about it? Are you going to enter the kitchen and bully the cook, telling him or her to speed up, so that you receive a partially cooked meal or something that's not even edible? So that you can brag to your friends how fast you "achieved your goal" (using the language of self-development), or in a LOA/spiritual language, "how fast you manifested your desires?"

No, while waiting for your order, you'll enjoy a glass of good wine, or whatever you want, while having fun and taking advantage of your time out leisurely. You can talk to your friends, and of course, you wouldn't stress out about their orders. You wouldn't compare your orders to theirs, because what they ordered is their choice, right? You know your order will come; now it's time to let go and relax.

While the example above was a metaphor, to make it more precise and easier to apply in real life, you need to balance out action and attraction. To be honest with you, this process is simple but not always easy, and there's no exact recipe for this, other than the recipe you create through your personal experience. The balance between action and attraction is always created by your energy, so whenever you speed up by taking action, that action must be taken from the energy of love and confidence, not from the energy of fear and lack. When you slow down and get into the energy of attraction, it's best to do so from the energy of peace and letting go, not from the energy of laziness, lack of patience, or entitlement to immediate results.

For example, you set the intention to manifest a new career, so that you can create more abundance while doing what you love. You balance action with attraction by sending your resumes and CV's to different companies, while at the same time, working on your energy and aligning yourself with the feeling of having your dream job. If you focus on mindless action, trying to send as many CV's as possible, without even researching the companies, you'd like to work for, and without aligning yourself with the feeling of having it now and living it in your mind, you may get stuck in a loop of just wanting and searching.

At the same time, if you just sit on your couch, visualize here and there, and don't take any action to get closer to your vision, it'll be hard, or even totally impossible to manifest your new career.

The word "action" is a part of the word "attraction". The law of attraction can help you align with the actions you need to take to get closer to your goals. The first part on your journey is aligning your energy and mindset with what you intend to manifest while being open to different suggestions from the Universe and willing to put in the work. As we already stated, when things don't go as planned, or there are some challenges on your way, see them as a part of the process because the Universe may want to test you.

Let's re-visit our example of manifesting your new career...

You take action when you actively research new companies you would like to work for, or any new direction you can take in your career. We live in the physical world, and so action is necessary. Regularly focusing on your thoughts, feeling and doing mindset work also involve taking action.

Then, you can let go, by focusing on gratitude, and feeling whole and complete because of what you already have. You can let go by taking care of your body, mind, and soul and doing what makes you feel good.

I know that sometimes, it's hard to let go, but as you practice what I suggest in this book, you'll eventually find your own balance, and your life will get much easier. From my personal observation, some people need to focus more on attraction, because they're already taking lots of action. Some people, on the other hand, focus too much on attraction or visualizing, but they don't take enough action to get closer to their goals.

I believe that readers can make their own judgments and decisions to figure out what they need to focus on now. We're in a constant state of flow.

For me personally, at this stage of my life, I focus more on attraction and inner work. It's because I've already taken action, and planted many seeds by taking action in the physical reality.

In other words, I worked hard to get skills I can monetize, and I created assets for myself. What was a real game-changer for me was slowing down and working on my energy, mindset, and spirituality.

Some people already mastered that spiritual part very well and perhaps need to focus more on taking action to manifest more abundance in this physical world. Do whatever you need to do, and change things up whenever required.

Ok, so now, let's have a look at some additional questions from readers.

Question:

Elena,

I'm definitely not where I want to be or who I want to be. But I'm getting used to appreciate my current state to transition to what I really want to manifest. Do you think it'll work for me if I let go? How fast?

Answer:

I cannot give you a definite answer as for what will work for you and how fast, because I am not you and I don't have all your answers. Also, your question is not very specific, and so I don't fully understand where you're coming from or where you're going. However, based on what you have written, I can give you some guidance. Take what you like and reject the rest.

First of all, the energy I get from your question is the energy of waiting or moving in circles. It's the energy of wanting; and if you want something, it means you don't have it. You also say you aren't where you want to be, and so the Universe listens to it and says: "OK, you aren't where you want to be, I listen to you, let's make it your default reality".

It'd be much better if you stated that you're in the process of manifesting your dreams, or you're in the process of aligning yourself with your new self-image.

Relax your mind and body to get some clarity. Then, instead of using words like "try" or "want", focus on "choosing" and "intending" – these are much more powerful.

I think it's good you're grateful and appreciative, as feelings of gratitude make you feel whole and complete. Keep going, keep learning, and your path and your true answers will unfold!

Question:

I'm still new to LOA and manifesting. Right now, I'm focused on deep understanding of how it works.

Someone who is into LOA, told me that if I focus on something I don't want in my life, like getting sick, for example, or losing my job, I'll manifest that into my life.

My problem is that I have horrible anxiety, and so whenever I try not to think about the negative, I end up thinking about it more.

I also have a lot of fears. I don't want to manifest them into my life either. Any tips for me?

Answer:

I can totally understand where you're coming from. I used to be a very anxious person, and so I struggled with the same thing on the outset of my personal LOA journey.

My advice would be to clear your mind with something like a guided meditation whenever you're feeling like you're focusing on negative thoughts.

At the same time, stay busy with what you're passionate about or what you love doing. It'll radically raise your vibration, reduce your anxiety, and give you more empowerment.

I think it's great you were able to diagnose what was holding you back at the beginning of your journey and had enough courage to reach out for guidance.

Everything will unfold for you just like it should. First, focus on your inner wellbeing and clearing your fears, doubts, and anxieties. Meditation is a fantastic healing modality to get into, and it's all free. When you feel like your energy and mindset begin to shift, start setting intentions to manifest small things and go from there to gain momentum and confidence.

We all have negative thoughts sometimes. I also do have them, but as long as I'm aware of them and can immediately make myself do something I enjoy or think about something I like, I'm all good.

Sometimes, you may have a bad day, but that doesn't mean you will manifest more bad days into your life. We're all humans, and nobody is perfect, LOA gurus also get negative thoughts, all of us do. The good thing is that we can transform negative into positive and turn the darkness into light. So, this is your journey, my friend.

Finally, remember that the law of attraction isn't so much about being scared of your negative thoughts. It's more about doing things and living in such a way that you feel good about it. That's all you need to do. Focus on what brings you happiness, and that will gradually rid you of all your anxieties.

Chapter 4 Center Your Mindset and Your Energy

Stay centered and focused on high vibration experiences instead of constantly comparing yourself to others.

I see this pattern all over again- new souls come to LOA, and they start off feeling very excited and hopeful. But, a few days pass, maybe even a few weeks, and they start questioning everything. They start comparing themselves to other people, who perhaps have been on this journey for a little longer and have already found ways to release their inner demons and subconscious blocks and so can manifest with more ease.

As a result, a new LOA soul starts to focus on the negative:

Why is it happening for me every time? I can't manifest, I can't achieve my goals, so maybe I'm not good enough!

Don't give your power away. Keep going! Why do you assume that the Universe doesn't want you to experience success, joy, love, abundance, and vibrant health? Stop judging yourself, stop giving yourself some stupid scores.

Many people visualize for three days and then just quit. This is the entry-level, kindergarten LOA (sorry, some tough love here, but this is how it is).

Instead, see and use LOA as a spiritual and self-development tool to create this new, more empowered version of yourself. Also, ask yourself if what you intend to manifest is genuinely your desire?

Sometimes we get stuck because we focus on manifesting a foreign goal. Perhaps you follow a career path that someone

59

recommended to you because it worked for him or her, but it's not for you?

For example, I love writing; I can write all day. And so, since I'm passionate about it, I can easily manifest more and more books. I'm an introvert by nature, and I enjoy the lifestyle that writing and publishing books gives me.

A good friend of mine got inspired, and she also wanted to become an author. But you see, it wasn't her real goal. She got interested in it because of freedom that the author's lifestyle can create, especially freedom of time and location. But, the writing wasn't for her; it made her feel drained; she didn't enjoy it at all!

However, we quickly realized she is passionate about designing and art. So, instead of writing, she decided to focus on creating covers and promotional designs for authors, and she loves it. In other words, she changed the channel of self-expression, and she focused on manifesting her own goal, not someone else's goal.

I can give you a massive feeling of freedom by saying this – allow yourself to get rid of extra weight that "trying to manifest" other people's goals may give you.

So, there you have it, another common manifestation mistake.

I've been guilty of it as well, and believe me when I say – when you manifest a foreign goal; it feels very lonely, and sad. You end up wondering: why? And you get stuck in this rat race of chasing this new thing to be happy.

I've met quite a few millionaires and multi-millionaires in my life: some were happy, and some were miserable; from my observation, those that were happy, were content because they were building companies and businesses they loved. They possessed that inner confidence that even if they lost it all, they could re-build themselves easily. Those that were miserable were building from a place of lack, trying to prove others wrong, or following other people's goals.

To be truly successful and happy in life, you need to clarify your true goals. That alone may take a few years of spiritual and personal development. So, if you still don't know what you really desire, set an intention to manifest your truth first and enjoy the process of going on a self-development journey!

It's good to build that foundation of authenticity in your life, have your values, and be honest with yourself. There's no point in chasing after something that's not even yours.

Now, if you already know exactly what your vision is, and you're manifesting and getting closer to your desire, but for some reason you feel like you're going too slow, let me tell you this...

Life happens in patterns and cycles. Certain things take a certain time. For example, it takes nine months to have a baby; it's not that we can speed up this process by expecting it to be only one month if we have nine women instead of one.

(It's a weird example, I know!)

But so often, we get caught up in wanting everything now as if it was a delivery from Amazon.

By the way, what seems so fast to us now, took years of work for Jeff Bezos and his teams to create, while everyone around him questioned what he was doing. Now, we can make an order from Amazon and enjoy it fast!

In nature, everything takes time. But now, we live in a world of instant gratification; this is what social media has done to us.

While there are so many benefits of using the internet and social media, there is also the downside. We want everything now, as fast as possible, and we also get too caught up in scrolling and comparing ourselves to other people.

This is why I took a very drastic move, and I'm not using social media. I went as far as deleting most of my profiles and will probably delete all of them. While I'm not saying this is the only way or you should do exactly what I do, who knows, perhaps, you will consider such a step if you think it's better for your long-term wellbeing.

Now, instead of scrolling and checking social media, I read, meditate, go for a walk, swim, or socialize. My life is so much better now. I know it works for me. More and more people are taking the same step I took, or are limiting the time they spent on scrolling. Remember that everything is energy, so even if you stay on social media, don't waste your time watching people whose energy you find harmful for some reason. Listen to your gut!

Oh, and finally, we've already talked about fear-based marketing, this is how most of the ads you see on social media are created and that energy can affect your manifestation unless you know how to protect your mind. Don't allow any negativity! Be patient and follow your process.

Whenever feeling impatient, remember that your manifestation process is like a movie, you just stop it and then come back to it. If you get tired of reading and need some sleep, you'll put this book down and carry on reading whenever you can. The book won't evaporate, right?

Once again, the attachment can drag you down if you think about the lack, but it can be great if you think about it, know it'll manifest sooner or later, and feel the emotion, the excitement that what you desire will manifest. It already exists, and it's making its way to your reality!

Get in that space and that vibration; right here, right now.

You don't need to be continually looking for new ways to manifest, especially if your energy needs a clean-up.

If you had what you wanted, would you still be desperately looking for new ways? Well, perhaps you would be exploring new ways to learn more if you're passionate about learning. But you wouldn't be desperate.

What would you be doing as the new 2.0 version of you that has already manifested your dreams?

Focus on your vision 100%, not only when you affirm or visualize, but also throughout the day. A person who does that and then decides to complain all day long, or gets impatient, well...

He or she hardly ever manifests anything good. It's all about the permanent energy and mindset shift.

Finally, you may sometimes feel tired or fed up with old ways or old avenues of expression. For example, as you shift your mindset and energy, perhaps you get tired of your current job and your current career. What used to be fun may be no longer fun, and now you're looking for something new, so that's fine.

Don't be afraid of testing and experimenting with new avenues of expression, any new ideas that come to your mind deserve to be explored.

All your manifestation goals, including your professional and personal goals, have an infinite number of ways to manifest. So, consider that and be open-minded about it.

Question:

Hi Elena!

Your emails make so much sense. I realized that I get some negative vibes from certain influencers I follow online, so I unfollowed them, and now I feel better. I spend more time in nature, and I have more time for self-care.

I stopped scrolling on social media! But my question is, how long will it take to stop judging myself and others? I still catch myself thinking about some people online and what they do.

Answer:

It takes one second, or less, to decide to stop judging, and that's already a high vibe decision. Then, just be mindful about it and stick to it. It may take time to build this "do not judge muscle." Focus on kindness and self-love, and the rest will follow.

As always, I'm unable to answer your question as to how long it would take. You need to ask your higher self, my friend! Focus on your new self-care routine and fill your free time with positive activities – exactly like you're doing now.

Question:

How do I act as I have it already? That always confuses me. How would I act if I met a dream guy or something?

Answer:

I can't tell you how to act because it's your life and your energy. From your question, I understand you intend to manifest a man into your life.

If I were you, I'd start playing your own manifestation detective, and ask yourself: "Would we live together? If yes, where? Where would we go out for dinners? Would he drive me to work? Would we live in a city or in a small town?"

But most importantly, how would he make you feel? Would he be like a fun guy, saying jokes, or maybe more of a serious guy? An introvert or extrovert? What kind of lifestyle would you live with him, and how would that make you feel?

Then, allow yourself that feeling right here and right now, but at the same time, feel whole and complete.

I hope this helps!

To sum up, when you find the emotion of your sincere desire and start feeling it, you just need to pretend you already have it. Recall that same emotion and let go of the obsession of desperately wanting and needing it so as not to push it away. The LOA encourages positivity and productivity, which will yield results; no matter what, you just need to keep going and allow yourself to be you.

It's a simple theory of reaction for every action.

True LOA also encourages you to become responsible for your life so that you can stop blaming others.

The problem is that some people think it's some magical mambo jumbo, and they can instantly manifest, even from a low vibration or negative energy.

(And yes they can manifest for sure, but very negative things, people and circumstances, I've been there myself!).

People in such a low vibe mindset usually think that they just need this new guru or this new technique, and they always repeat the same old pattern of desperately trying new techniques.

Well, self-development is a life-long journey, and it does require work as well as building new muscles. LOA is one of the modalities of self-development, and as a modality, it has different schools of thought and different practices. None is right or wrong; instead, it's all about understanding who you are and what you truly desire to manifest and to stay true to your vision through your thoughts, actions, and feelings.

For me, the biggest challenge I faced was blaming, attacking, and criticizing others. The biggest realization came when I realized I was getting close to becoming an online bully! Then, I got very sick, which made me re-evaluate my life, my energy, my businesses, and everything. So, I turned back to LOA and gratitude. I made a promise to myself that I'd never waste my life away in negativity because life is too short for that.

At the same time, it isn't my intention to fight negativity and negative people. It's their life and their choices; I'm nobody to judge them because I've no idea what's going on in their souls and minds.

If they're ready to change, they'll attract the inspiration and tools they need. You can't be a Robin Hood for everyone, as it'll really drain your energy and lower your vibration. So, focus on your journey!

Question:

I wish all my friends were like you Elena; I'd love to talk to positive people. I live in a small town and even though I'm grateful for my old friends like we went to school together and all that, now that I'm on this self-development journey and also expanding as an empath, I feel like I have a bigger purpose. I'd like to become a life coach (I almost finished my certification) or a motivational speaker. I've already manifested some speaking gigs and coaching sessions. But my old friends don't get it, and I feel like it affects my energy, what do I do then?

Answer:

I can't tell you what to do, I can't tell you to leave your friends, nor can I ask you to stick to them.

I can only encourage you to be yourself. Not everyone is into life coaching or law of attraction. I understand this journey can be lonely. If you feel that your old friends are negative about it, just don't talk about it. You can discuss things you used to chat about together, granted you all still have an interest in them.

The most important thing is happiness, and people find it in different ways. I know many people who are not into LOA, but are still lovely and kind people.

So, do your own thing, focus on your journey. There are many online groups where you can talk to people about your new passion – LOA, and coaching, and you can also create a meet up in your local area. I wouldn't focus that much on people you think are negative. Focus on people who get you and give you good vibes!

Personally, I avoid topics such as LOA, self-development, or spirituality whenever I hang out with people who are not into it or have no idea what that is. Unless they ask me, or I feel they need help, I don't talk about it. I can make an exception if someone needs my help, or it makes sense to open one's eyes to it. In other circumstances, I just enjoy the moment and individual energy of different people while taking an interest in what they do in life. Hope this helps! You don't need to feel lonely on your journey, my friend.

Chapter 5 Do You Speak, Think, and Act to Manifest? Or Do Block Your Manifestations Without Even Knowing?

Your language patterns are extremely important, and there are many words I highly recommend you choose to let go of accordingly.

It may take some time, but it's worth it, especially when you start applying the tools from this chapter so that you know exactly which words to use instead.

We're talking about words that are extremely powerful and will make you feel confident and empowered while amplifying and speeding up the manifestation process.

For example, instead of saying:

"I am trying to",

say:

"I am playing," or "I am experimenting."

To say that you try automatically allows the huge possibility of failure and even a lack of genuine commitment. For example, instead of saying: "I am trying this new business idea," I prefer to say: "I am experimenting with this new opportunity, or I am learning about it."

You see, when you experiment or learn, there's no space to fail.

When you experiment, you get a result that will teach you something. There's no such thing as a negative outcome; it's just an outcome, which is some kind of valuable feedback and data.

Instead of saying: "I want to," say:

"I choose to, or: "I intend to." Both are much more powerful!

Wanting makes us all wannabes. By definition, a wannabe wants something because he or she doesn't have it. If you're a pro at something, you already have it, and you do it. It's absolutely normal for you.

You can also say that you're in the process of manifesting something. Expressing that you are in the process is an excellent way to help you reduce resistance. This is extremely helpful if you set big goals and massive intentions, and maybe you get a bit nervous. If you state that you're in the process, it'll calm you down, almost on autopilot.

Move on with clarity and be decisive. For example, if you desire to become a successful entrepreneur, focus on one venture until successful. You can't be halfway in, and halfway out.

By the way, I used to be a "half-wayer," lol, don't even get me started! But once I've made a clear decision and focused on my passion, things began to change, and I started manifesting people and circumstances that would help me.

Also, avoid "maybes" and "when I get this, then I'll..." thought patterns. Why not get there directly?

Maybe there's a direct flight?

Alignment is vital, since you don't want to be in chaos vibrations; or you don't want to manifest "maybes" or "I'll do this when..." situations.

How do you know how to make the right decision?

Well, I can't tell you precisely since I can't make any decision for you. You see, I used to let other people decide for me, and then, whenever I manifested what I didn't want, I'd blame them, not myself. I want to stay away from such energy. Making decisions is also a muscle. Follow your gut!

Be specific, don't be vague, this is where visualizations can help, you can visualize as a tool to help you "taste your new reality" to see what you like and how you feel. You can also visualize to stretch your mindset and realize where your fears or weak points are to let them go.

Reverse engineer by thinking about the amazing things you've achieved so far: I'm sure you were specific, and that idea just came to your mind, and you just knew it was the right thing to do. Reverse engineering what already worked for you is one of the best tools, because you and your own life are your best mentors, seriously!

There's a simple exercise you can do for daily clarity and alignment. It can be done in 5-10 minutes.

It'll help you attune to the energy of the new work and people you want to manifest into your life.

Please note, journaling and scripting can't be done from a place of scarcity. It's not about how much time you spend writing in your journal, or what kind of journal you use. Just like it's not about how many vision boards you make and how long you visualize for. It's all about your feeling and the emotion behind it. Yes, sometimes, you may find yourself feeling like a robot. Just be aware of it and focus on something that makes you feel good, dance or do some quick yoga pose.

You attract who you are; so if you feel empty, then you'll attract like. Keep your mind and soul open to different sensations.

Ask yourself when you would like to manifest your desire? While I'm not too big on obsessing about deadlines, I'm all about patience and being OK with waiting for a bit longer; it's also good to create some kind of a timeline or a deadline.

As I was de-cluttering my house, I found an old vision board and mission statement, where I wrote down, I'd be living close to a beach, somewhere on the Atlantic; I had no idea how it'd happen, but it felt authentic to me, very authentic.

It said, by the end of 2023. Well, now it's 2020, and I've achieved this goal. A friend of mine, whom I met entirely on accident, was going traveling and offered me his property in the Canary Islands. And I'm still here looking after it. I don't own this property, but it just came to me, and I can experience living here. My original request didn't say that I'd own a house somewhere overlooking the Atlantic; it meant I would be living in one.

Now, when I think about it, I should have been more specific, haha! I guess a part of me feared owning such property for some reason, and so now I'm clearing that out.

I'm very happy. I know it's already unfolding, and living here, I get to experience this vibration. I know the next step will come; in the meantime, I'm happy that I'm getting closer!

Ever since, it conceived in my mind; I knew I had to align my actions, feelings, and thoughts. And I'd regularly write it in my journal as if it'd already happen. It was also a fantastic manifestation for me to experience healing, transform my health, and learn a new culture.

Last year I began journaling about the new gate opening for me and manifesting unexpected income. Well, it came to me through a tax refund and an amazing deal with an audiobook publishing company.

I just kept writing in my journal that I'm ready to let go of control, and I'm now open to manifesting unexpected income from unexpected sources. That's it. I let go of being so logical.

The thing I focus on now is manifesting more friends, social life, and happy moments. It's already unfolding very well, and I am very excited for what's yet to come. This process works for all areas of life, not just for material manifestations.

Please note, I'm not saying this to brag. I merely aim to inspire you to show you that it works, if you genuinely intend to make it work. Also, some people may prefer another method such as vision boards and looking at them while feeling the emotion. Personally, I love writing, journaling, and scripting. Like I said, I'm a journaling junkie! I buy a ton of journals, and I love them all.

But, as always, what works for me, may not be the best for all my readers. So, I like to give you different options to explore.

Some people prefer to record themselves and then listen to their intentions, it's like audio scripting! And it works for many of my friends. But I prefer scripting and journaling.

If you wanted to practice all the methods every day, you would go mad and create resistance. You're better off picking just one way, going all in, really feeling it, and eventually creating a variation of it that works for you.

So, from now on, focus on feelings and emotions. These work for affirmations, journaling, and visualizations, as well as for vision boards.

You don't manifest what you want to manifest. You manifest what you are. Who you are is made of your energy, mindset, and feelings.

Whenever practicing any manifestation method, what I highly recommend is to first be in high vibration or meditate beforehand.

After you do that, get clear on what you intend to manifest. Then, you can visualize, write, or affirm, whatever works for you. Whatever you choose to do, make sure to include lots of emotional words, words that make you feel good, and give you an emotional high. Deeply feel the emotions while doing so. Finally, just let it go and move on your daily activities with good energy.

Using different manifestation methods isn't meant to obtain something for you. Manifestation methods are used in order to tune your vibration and become a vibrational match to your desire.

If you're practicing any manifestation method every day because you're feeling anxious or impatient about your desire, then you'll massively put off your success ...So, use any manifestation method you choose to use, to feel good about your desire.

When I do my gratitude journaling or my scripting, I do it because it feels good to me, and I enjoy living in the moment of mindfully putting my desires on paper. Then, I know I'm on a vibrational match to it.

So, to answer the most common question I get, which is: *how often do I need to affirm, visualize, or journal?*

I'd advise: do them as often or as little as you want as long as it feels good to do so. Create a habit you enjoy! It may take a while to experiment with different methods and to see which one you like.

It's OK to do so as long as you aren't acting from the energy of desperation (such as: "Oh I need to find my method today and manifest till tomorrow").

Everything I do, I first ask myself about my energy. Sometimes I get tense when writing. Not just physically tense, but mentally, emotionally, and even spiritually tense. I see it as a sign of resistance; my body is trying to tell me something. So, I take a break from writing, and I focus on relaxation, meditation, or relaxing my energy. Then, I get back to writing. New ideas just flow, I feel good, and I can create better books for you to enjoy.

Here are more questions from our readers:

Hi Elena,

I have a question about journaling and scripting. So, do I just write about the experiences that I want to have? Because I don't really want anything materialistic. I want to manifest health and happiness. How do I do it the right way?

Answer:

There's really no "wrong" way to journal anything; it's different for everyone. Just make sure you're writing in the present tense as if you're currently living the life you want and feel the emotions while you do it. Be specific about the happy moments you intend to manifest. For example:"Every weekend, I enjoy amazing parties in beautiful locations. I eat sophisticated dinners with interesting people. I laugh and have fun."

Or: "Every evening, I hang out with my kids, and we laugh and play."

Manifesting isn't just about money; even if a person wants to manifest financial abundance, the subconscious mind finds it hard to understand the money and numbers; however, it can easily align with the feeling of freedom and happiness.

At the same time, many of my readers who tried to manifest abundance for years (yea they tried and nothing happened), suddenly began manifesting unexpected income, just by focusing on manifesting happiness first.

Some food for thought!

I can personally attest to the holistic effectiveness of focusing on manifesting happiness and peace of mind. The rest becomes easier, and all the resistance gets removed.

Question:

My whole life I never know what I want. I'm 49 and still don't know. I have no idea what direction to take and no clue what specifically I desire to manifest. Any tips?

Answer:

Release the grip and the pressure you put on yourself to figure it out. Be a happy flower for now!

What makes you happy? Well, do it more often! You may also explore different paths of raising your vibration just for the sake of it, it really feels good. I have a free five-day program aimed at helping you raise your vibration, and you can find it at the end of this book and on my website:

www.LOAforSuccess.com

By raising your vibration, you also change your energy, mindset, and perspective. I'm very positive that the answers may come to you automatically as soon as you focus on working on your vibration.

Question:

So, I know what I want, but I was also told to stay open-minded in case it doesn't happen for me. Am I blocking what I really want?

Answer:

I've no idea whether you're blocking what you intend to manifest because I'm not your higher self. I don't have your deep answers. However, I am very positive that you aren't blocking anything by staying open-minded, reducing the importance and taking action from a place of love. As long as you focus on your energy and take action from a place of love, peace, and confidence, you'll do very well on your journey.

Personally, I'm a big fan of the approach you follow, and it's something I've learned from the book: Reality Transurfing by Vladim Zeland (one of my favorite books to be honest). I've found success with manifesting by using this approach, and I also got rid of anxiety and insomnia, so it all worked very well for me.

Many personal development gurus or business gurus will tell you to go all-in and hustle and grind while burning all the bridges. I also tried this approach in my old life, and it did not work for me very well. I've seen people become very successful using such a plan, but many have also paid for success with their health, happiness, and personal relationships; and for me, it wouldn't be worth it.

Chapter 6 Finally Remove Resistance, Fears, and Blocks

Have you ever felt like you are applying LOA and manifesting some things but feel like there's no regularity, or you can never manifest your more significant things, only smaller things?

Maybe you failed in the past, or someone said something that really stuck in your subconscious mind.

When you experience resistance, it's harder to manifest your desires. You feel as if you were carrying some carry bags on your shoulders while having some heavyweights tied to your legs.

The more you try, the harder it gets. You may learn some new techniques on how to walk and run, but still, it'll be hard!

So, releasing resistance can be helpful, and there are many simple tools you can use. In fact, you can start right now!

Conscious Breathing

Keep breathing and affirming that you're releasing your resistance and letting go. You'll immediately feel peaceful, especially if you set a firm intention that you'll remove your resistance.

You can say it out loud or just think it to yourself. You can breathe in through your nose and breathe out through your mouth. You can also breathe in through your mouth and release it through your mouth.

Do it whenever you're feeling stressed out, and add it to your manifestation toolbox through what I like to call, the manifestation habit stacking.

Manifestation Habit Stacking

The manifestation habit stacking is when you incorporate resistance-reducing activities into any daily habits, such as making tea, having a shower, or even brushing your teeth.

Another way is to utilize your time in the shower. Take a shower with a firm intention of letting go; use the power of water. You've probably experienced it before, for example, on the beach. The sound of water is potent and healing itself.

Even listening to guided meditations with the sounds of water, can be very healing!

Use your cleaning time, whenever you are cleaning your house and removing the rubbish, set the intention that you are also removing your old emotional garbage. It'll allow you to speak directly to your subconscious mind and make a fantastic connection.

As you can see, the above techniques are very easy. They don't require learning anything new, and you don't need to purchase any fancy technology.

Most people get used to living with resistance, and so it becomes their default state, along with stress and anxiety. They don't even question it. Resistance becomes their personality, which then becomes their personal reality. Exactly as Doctor Joe Dispenza teaches in all his books, such as in his book *Breaking the Habit of Being Yourself*; your personality is your personal reality!

(I highly recommend his books, by the way, since they offer excellent information!).

By regularly doing the exercises I share in this chapter, you'll also experience more energy, life force, and inner peace as positive side effects. I also recommend you focus on removing resistance before doing any manifestation techniques (visualizations, affirmations, journaling, scripting, gratitude). With removed resistance, or at least reduced resistance, you'll be able to take everything you do to the next level.

Also, do the exercises to remove resistance before any income-generating activities, such as calling clients, talking to your boss, doing a presentation, or any activities that are relevant to your work or business. First of all, you'll feel happier and much more relaxed. Then, your energy will shift, and so you'll be able to attract more high vibe people and thoughts into your life. When you feel good, you usually crave more of what makes you feel good.

It's like an addictive fast food for the mind, with the only difference— it's right for you, and there's no reason to cut back on it. You can never over do the feel good stuff; and even if you did, you could always radiate it to people around you who might need some positivity.

Removing resistance will also give you more clarity, and your intentions will be much stronger. After I began removing resistance from my body, I stopped eating fast food, and now I love cooking healthy and nutritious meals.

So, let's revisit removing resistance. Personally, I like to set a short 5-minute meditation a day as a way to align with my vision and remove resistance. The primary purpose of my practice is releasing old patterns and negative energies that are holding me back. All you need is intuitive breathing and consistency.

You can also try to tighten all your muscles and then relax them. Repeat a few times, while focusing on the parts of your body that are the most tense. It works like magic and helps to keep negative thoughts away.

I used to struggle with visualization. Another problem I faced was that as someone who would often get anxious and worried, I'd often begin to visualize negative situations from the past while replaying some old programs in my mind.

However, once I focused on releasing resistance, everything changed for me. Suddenly visualizing was so much fun for me and opened the gateway to manifesting incredible people and circumstances into my life.

This chapter contains all you need to help you remove resistance while eliminating energy blocks, doubts, and fears.

It's that simple. However, if you feel you'd like to dive deeper, I highly recommend you check out EFT (Emotional Freedom Technique). A good book on this topic I'd suggest is *The Tapping Solution* by Nick Ortner.

What I love about the EFT, is that once you've learned the basics, it'll always be with you, and you can use it whenever you want, even when you travel.

As for extra tips for helping you reach a relaxed state while eliminating resistance, I'd suggest a few natural remedies such as:

-Lavender essential oil – the best way to use it is with an aromatherapy vaporizer while meditating. You can add a few drops to your bath (and add a bit of coconut oil to it), or add a few drops to a natural body lotion or natural body oil. Lavender massage is very relaxing and soothing for the body and mind. It'll also help you sleep better!

You may experiment with fennel and chamomile essential oil. All essential oils are great to raise your vibration.

-herbal teas and infusions such as fennel tea, chamomile tea, or valerian tea (be sure to consult with a natural health professional first because some people are allergic to certain herbs, and herbs may also interfere with some medications).

-Bach Flower Remedies – to obtain the best results with Bach Flower remedies, you would need to talk to a certified Bach Flower therapist, who could advise the best Bach Flower remedy for your specific fears. You can also go for the Rescue Bach Flower Remedy, which, as the name suggests is a natural remedy aimed at offering you a deep relief of your fears. In some countries, you can buy the Rescue Bach flower remedy in a pharmacy or a health food store. You can also find it online and on Amazon.

-Ashwagandha – this ancient Ayurvedic remedy is also excellent to help you soothe your nerves, sleep better, get better rest, and reduce tension and anxiety.

Remember that resistance creates more resistance. Resistance is based on fears and insecurities. Let them go! At the same time, accept them. The worst thing you could do is start blaming yourself for experiencing resistance while adding another negative pattern. Nope, say, thank you very much!

It's time to let go of what no longer serves you and focus on the new, empowered chapter of your life. Your old, self-manifested resistance may have popped up as you went back to negativity, and you're seeing some shadows of it now. It's normal, nothing to worry about. However, what matters is the now!

Now, your new self is manifesting some really amazing things, and with so many good things happening around you, there's no more place for negativity.

You've manifested this book and this chapter for a reason, so how about that for a starter? Just be open and notice how the energy, the vibration, and everything around you can massively change. You're a new, resistance-free person now!

Question:

How often should I check my energy and resistance?

Answer:

Whenever you need! Just be mindful about it. As always, awareness is vital to success!

Chapter 7 Forget Your Past Mistakes and Create Your Inner Freedom

Don't dwell on the past. The past is done, especially if you've experienced any negative manifestations, if you had financial issues in the past, or couldn't manifest your love. Don't focus on that, don't think too much about it, and don't talk about it.

If any anxious thoughts arise, don't stress about them, just say to yourself: *Oh, thanks for the reminder, the NOW is so much better!*

You only have the present moment and what is now. It doesn't matter what happened in the past because you were a different person then. Focus on what's happening now and what can give you good feelings right now, so that you can create a beautiful future.

Target good feelings about money, abundance, love, health, and energy. Be grateful for every small manifestation. Don't take anything for granted. You made a delicious smoothie, that blend came up amazing? Be grateful! First of all, you had the ingredients. Someone had to work hard to create them for you! You also had a blender, a fantastic device that helps you live a healthy lifestyle.

Did you manifest a dollar? Once again, be grateful. Even if something didn't go your way today, remember, you aren't failing, you're learning, and life is your best teacher. As Abraham says, we're here on Earth to experience contrasts; and, in my opinion, we should be grateful for that too! We can experience all those fantastic moments because we have also experienced the contrast.

So, even if something doesn't go your way now, find something to be grateful for! Now you're getting direct lessons from the Universe, and these free lessons are meant to align your energy with what you truly desire. Focus on feeling good now and enjoy the now.

If you're in the present moment and focus on gratitude, there's no space for mindless wanting. This is the best state for attracting!

When you want something very badly (just like I wanted to manifest more money fast, and I kept telling the Universe I wasn't enough), you're in a vibration of lack. At the same time, negative beliefs about money or other things we intend to manifest, are like extra emotional baggage preventing us from moving forward.

But, when you focus on the here and now and do a quick gratitude exercise, the negativity and low vibes go away. The more gratitude you practice for the here and now, and the more blessings you notice around you, the higher your vibration!

On the contrary, if you keep wanting and needing, it shows that you don't have it. You keep affirming the lack.

I remember, many years ago, when I was still new to LOA (although my ego kept telling me I knew it all because I'd read a few books, haha), and I really wanted to see a Tony Robbins' event in London. So, I kept writing it all over again in my manifestation journal. I wanted to manifest tickets or some unexpected money to be able to go to that event.

Even though at that time, I was in a well-paid position, working in sales for an international company, I'd always manifest unexpected expenses and still struggled with money.

The more I wanted, the less I could manifest, especially since that I was in a very needy mindset. So, nothing happened, and I didn't manifest a ticket to the Tony Robbins' event.

Eventually, I got very frustrated and decided to give up.

However, now, I am very grateful for this experience because it taught me what didn't work.

You see, I mindlessly kept writing: "I want to manifest tickets to Tony Robbins". And, yes, I manifested more WANTING!

A couple of years later, I decided to give the law of attraction another go. I began reading Esther Hicks, and I mindfully intended to manifest tickets to one of her seminars. I could still remember how I couldn't manifest the tickets or money to see Tony Robbins. However, I didn't want that to stop me. I decided to reframe it as a learning experience to be able to manifest eventually.

I decided to let go of my past mistakes and focus on the now. We learn from the past, but to dwell on it can make us stuck. So, focus on the now, and this is how you'll create your future.

The first thing I did was to let go of needy expectations and what author Vladim Zeland (once again, I highly recommend his book *Reality Transurfing*) calls "Excess potential."

So, I said to myself, wow, Elena, you can always learn from Esther's books, online courses, and even free videos and free articles. There's so much abundance for you already and a wealth of wisdom for you to absorb to help you live a better life!

So, I created a desire from this energy. I felt happy and abundant, knowing that even if I didn't manifest the tickets, I could still learn and grow. I also set the intention for the unexpected to enter and allow me to see Abraham Hicks live.

I asked myself: *Elena, how would you act if you could easily afford to buy a ticket to Abraham Hicks and also pay for a nice hotel and nice dinners to hang out with amazing people? Would you stress out about it? Would you write how badly you want it? Would you even stress out about the date when you must, should and need to receive it? Of course not. If anything, you'd be writing how grateful you feel for ALREADY, manifesting your intentions.*

I really enjoyed the process, felt good about it, and grew my Manifestation Muscle. As a result, an old friend of mine messaged me and told me she had a spare ticket to Abraham's event. I also manifested an unexpected bonus and was able to stay in a nice hotel, met great people at the event, and enjoyed a super high vibration. After sharing my story with one of the people I met at the event, I started crying from joy.

The feeling was so familiar - I said: *It's all happening exactly like I wanted.*

The new friend I made at the event confirmed:

Well, you have practiced the feeling many times, this is how it works, I have done it many times, I teach this stuff, and my clients use it successfully. Once you've got the hang of it and stick to it, it always works as long as you use it for the good things that serve you and others.

Even if the law of attraction doesn't work for you now, know that your time will come! You're practicing the feeling; you're practicing for the bigger show!

It's like losing weight; you go step by step—the same with raising your salary or business revenue.

So, stay in the flow, and relax your soul! Finally, remember, what seems complicated for you now, is easy for the Universe.

It's about your personal empowerment, creativity, and nourishment. It's about planting your manifestation seed. Speak to it and nourish it! If you realize it wasn't your seed, there's no problem; because with LOA, you always get a new, fresh chance, and you can always try again.

Now, let's talk a bit about visualization, or to be more precise, how not to visualize. We've already discussed visualization as a tool to stretch your mindset, feel good, and remove resistance. In the next chapter, we'll focus on the most common mistakes people make while visualizing, to make sure you create the visualization process that always works for you.

Chapter 8 How Not to Visualize

When visualizing, the main intention should be to release resistance, not to create more of it. The good thing is that when you visualize, your brain is getting primed in a compelling way while creating reference experiences, right now in the present moment.

This practice works excellent for re-programming your subconscious mind. As with all the manifestation techniques, you need the feeling you can align with your mind and heart, too!

The most common mistake people make when visualizing is that they see themselves in a movie, from a third person. What it does is that you don't identify yourself with it, and it's harder to manifest. You're separating yourself rather than fusing yourself with your vision.

It's much better to imagine it through your eyes.

Also, visualization is not about some external point in the future. You have the power to make yourself feel any emotion you want right here right now. Visualize things that make you feel good, feel proud of yourself. Visualizing the process is also very powerful – so practice your new, empowered version. Fuse yourself with it to practice your unique vibration and align yourself with it.

Stay in that vibration in your everyday activities. Your old apartment can be treated like your own villa if you regard it as such. When you check your bank account and see, let's say $2000, imagine it's $20,000, or $200,000. Imagine it's there, and it's safe, you're safe. It's normal for you to make, keep, spend, and invest money. Money always comes to you, and it replenishes easily. Money likes you.

If you want to manifest a healthy, fit body, and you run one mile a day, imagine you can run five or even ten miles! In other words, use everyday routines and situations to trick your brain into thinking:

It's already happening, and it's something normal for me!

Imagine a person whose desire is to be a well-known stand-up comedian who gets a small local gig, but there are only 30 people in the audience. But, the person can choose to pretend that there are 300 people or even 3,000 people, why not?

Another person wants to lose 20 pounds and already lost 2 pounds. Well, they can pretend they've lost 10 or 12 pounds already!

Your brain is a machine that loves getting clear signals. Communicate with it through emotions and visualizations. Your brain LOVES such games!

Question:

I struggle with visualizing from the first person, but I'm working hard to change that already :) I want to manifest a six-figure position in my company. I'm very close as I recently got a significant promotion.

I've been following your books and emails for a few months now, and they empowered me. I know that LOA works, and a recent promotion (even though it's still not my big goal) feels like the first step on my manifestation journey.

So, I want to keep practicing visualization. I try to focus on my new office, new business meetings, but it's a bit blurry, and I can't fully feel it. Any tips to make it easier and faster with my visualization?

Answer:

The best tip is to focus on the things you love doing. Seriously! You need to ask yourself why you intend to manifest that six-figure job. What drives you?

Is it the prestige and recognition at your company? Your dedication and hard work? If yes, keep visualizing the work you'd do and focus on the process and how you enjoy it.

If however, your desire to manifest a six-figure salary is because you want to improve your lifestyle, focus on the freedom the money can give you.

For example, exotic travels, shopping, eating at nice restaurants. How would you think as a six-figure earner? How would you manage your money? Would you invest? Would you have an accountant? Again, there's no reason to overthink if it makes you feel confused. Stick to the questions that make you feel good, and excited and use them as a foundation for your visualizations. Whatever makes you feel good!

Question:

Can you teach me how to stop thinking about someone all the time? That person is draining my energy. I try not to, but I still think about him, and I hate it. I want to let go of that person and move on.

Answer:
Practise meditation. You won't believe me, but I was just like you. I, too used to overthink and could not let go. Relax. Meditate. Visualize you are all by yourself in beautiful locations. It always works! Also, don't get too caught up in trying. Focus more on mindful visualization.

Question:

There are many opportunities I'd like to manifest to become a multi-entrepreneur, with different streams of income, but I'm not so sure which one I should pick first. I assume it's better to manifest one specific thing and only then do something else? So, how do I begin visualizing? Should I start from the most lucrative opportunity?

Answer:

Focus more on what you are passionate about, and then those things will all come as a side effect. Money is a side-effect of us doing our passion while being of service to others etc.

For example, several years ago, I'd visualize myself doing videos and selling expensive programs and retreats. I thought it was the only way because I saw other people manifest abundance doing it.

However, I had no passion for it at all. I'm a writer at my core, and this is my authentic self. I spent about three years, visualizing what was not for me to begin with.

As a result, I could never get it. The Universe kindly refused because it wasn't for me; there was a much better path for me. So, if visualization doesn't work for you now, it can also mean you aren't passionate about what you want, and something better, much better, will unfold for you. So, you can't lose my friend; you can only win!

Conclusion

The law of attraction is the real phenomena, and you'll find millions upon millions of law of attraction success stories.

At the same time, many people give up because it didn't work for them right away, or they came across some subconscious blocks (whether they knew it or not).

What's of paramount importance is your perception. See the LOA and manifestation process as a long-term tool to help you align with your higher self and embrace positivity for good.

Use it to focus on your energy, health, and happiness while letting go of old fears and doubts. Grow your manifestation muscle.

Yes, perhaps you didn't get that promotion now, maybe subconsciously you had a fear, maybe you even feared making more money (even though consciously you thought you "wanted it"). You can perceive it as something negative, such as: *Oh, LOA did not work.*

Or you can see it something positive, be your own LOA detective, and focus on learning more about yourself.

Some people sign up for a gym, and because of their excellent genetics and perfect metabolism may get amazing results fast, even though they skip sessions here and there, and their diet isn't perfect.

At the same time, some people need more time and work to achieve similar results, even with the best nutrition and workout plan out there.

FINAL WORDS

There's no point in comparing yourself to other people. Everyone has a different journey and karma to face. You don't fail, you succeed, or you learn more about yourself.

Challenges and obstacles have only one purpose. They make you re-wire your brain and transform your self-image.

They happen for you, not to you.

They're a part of the process! The Universe wants to test you to see how strong your intentions are. The Universe may ask you to confirm your order. It isn't a big deal!

The Universe might be sending you some obstacles here and there to make you leave your comfort zone or re-align your path, so that you can manifest your vision and create long-term success in all areas of your life.

You're reading this book and its final pages for a reason. Never limit your dreams because of some initial setbacks.

The Universe is just testing you and giving you some awesome tools for you to grow.

Just tune in and listen.

Stay strong, my friend! I hope we "meet" again in another book.

Remember - I love you, I believe in you, and I pray for you!

Thank you for reading this little book until the very end!

Now, before you go, I'd love your feedback!

So, if you have any thoughts to share about this book, please post a review on Amazon and Good Reads.

It doesn't have to be long if you're busy; in fact, just one sentence will do.

Your review can also help other readers in our community avoid the most common manifestation mistakes and get closer to their dreams.

I love hearing from my readers and I'm eager to read your review.

Thank you, and have a beautiful day!

PS. To stay in touch with me, my latest author updates and new releases, follow my website and my Amazon page at:

www.LOAforSuccess.com

www.amazon.com/author/elenagrivers

Until next time, much love!

Free LOA Newsletter + Bonus Gift

To help you AMPLIFY what you've learned in this book, I'd like to offer you a free copy of my ***LOA Workbook – a powerful, FREE 5-day program (eBook & audio)*** designed to help you raise your vibration while eliminating resistance and negativity.

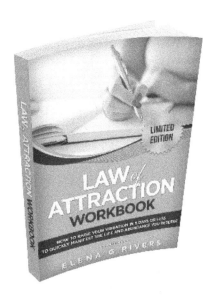

To sign up for free, visit the link below now:

www.loaforsuccess.com/newsletter

You'll also get free access to my highly acclaimed, uplifting **LOA Newsletter.**

Through this email newsletter, I regularly share all you need to know about the manifestation mindset and energy.

My newsletter alone helped hundreds of my readers manifest their own desires.

Plus, whenever I release a new book, you can get it at a deeply discounted price or even for free.

You can also start receiving my new audiobooks published on Audible at no cost!

To sign up for free, visit the link below now:

www.loaforsuccess.com/newsletter

I'd love to connect with you and stay in touch with you while helping you on your LOA journey!

If you happen to have any technical issues with your sign up, please email us at:

support@LOAforSuccess.com

More Books by Elena G.Rivers

Available on Amazon – eBook, paperback and hardcover editions are not available for your convenience

(just search for "Elena G.Rivers" in your local Amazon Store) For more information visit author's website at:

www.LOAforSuccess.com

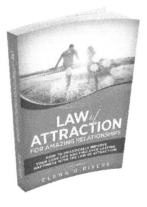

The Money Mindset Audiobook is now available on Audible!

For more information, visit:

www.LOAforSuccess.com/audiobooks